Muppet Babies

Coloring Book

Kevin Barnett

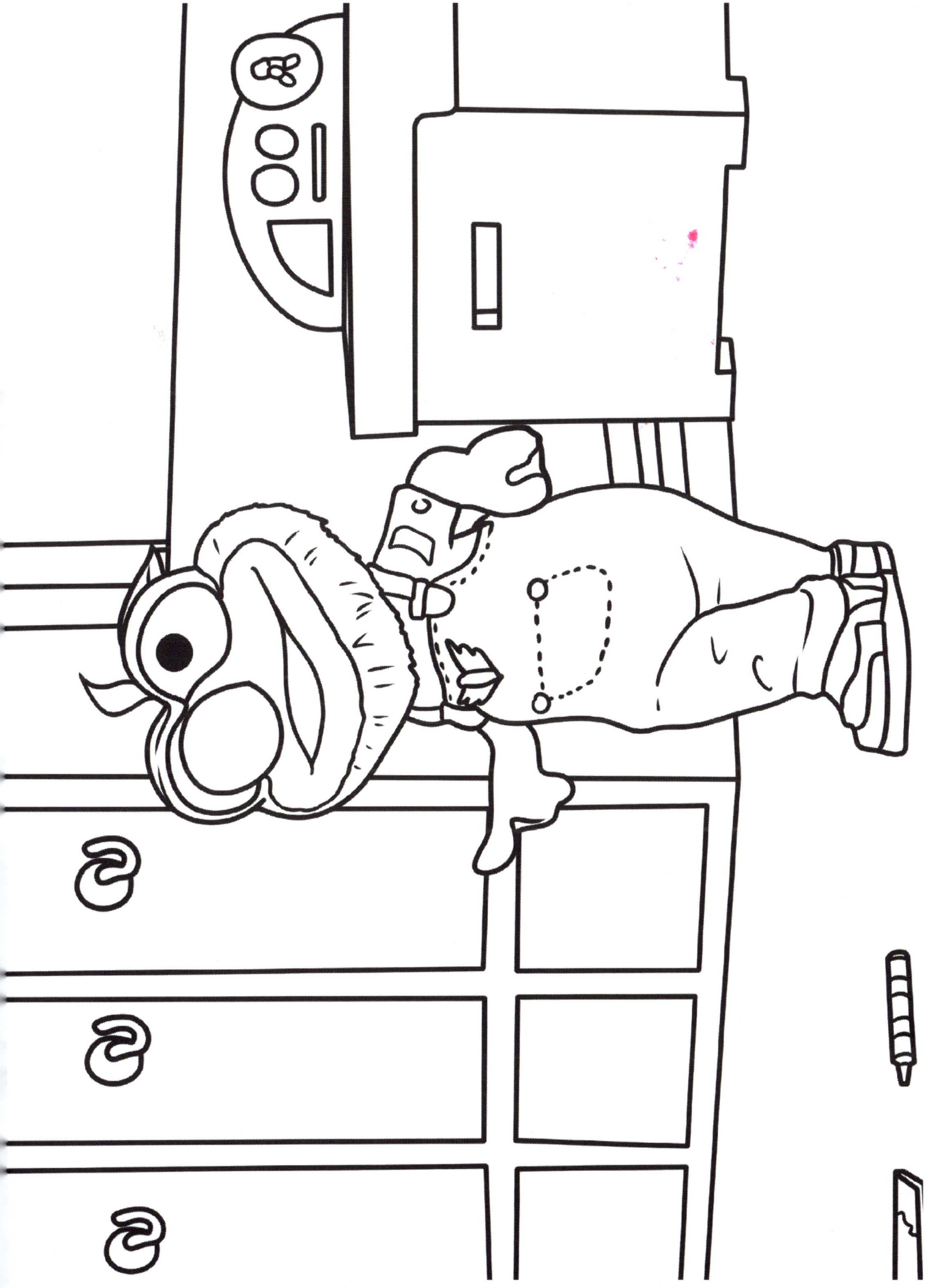

Z

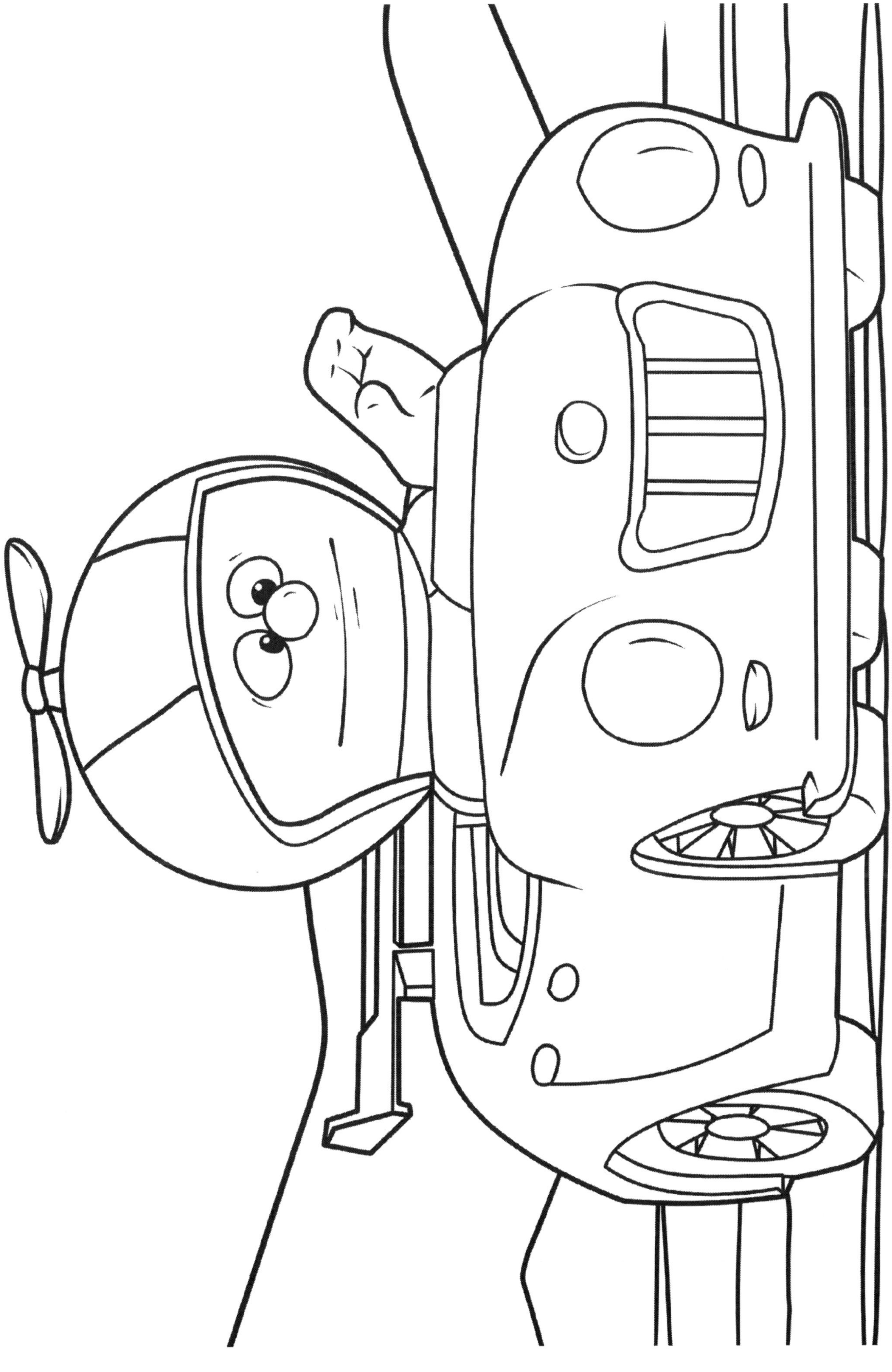

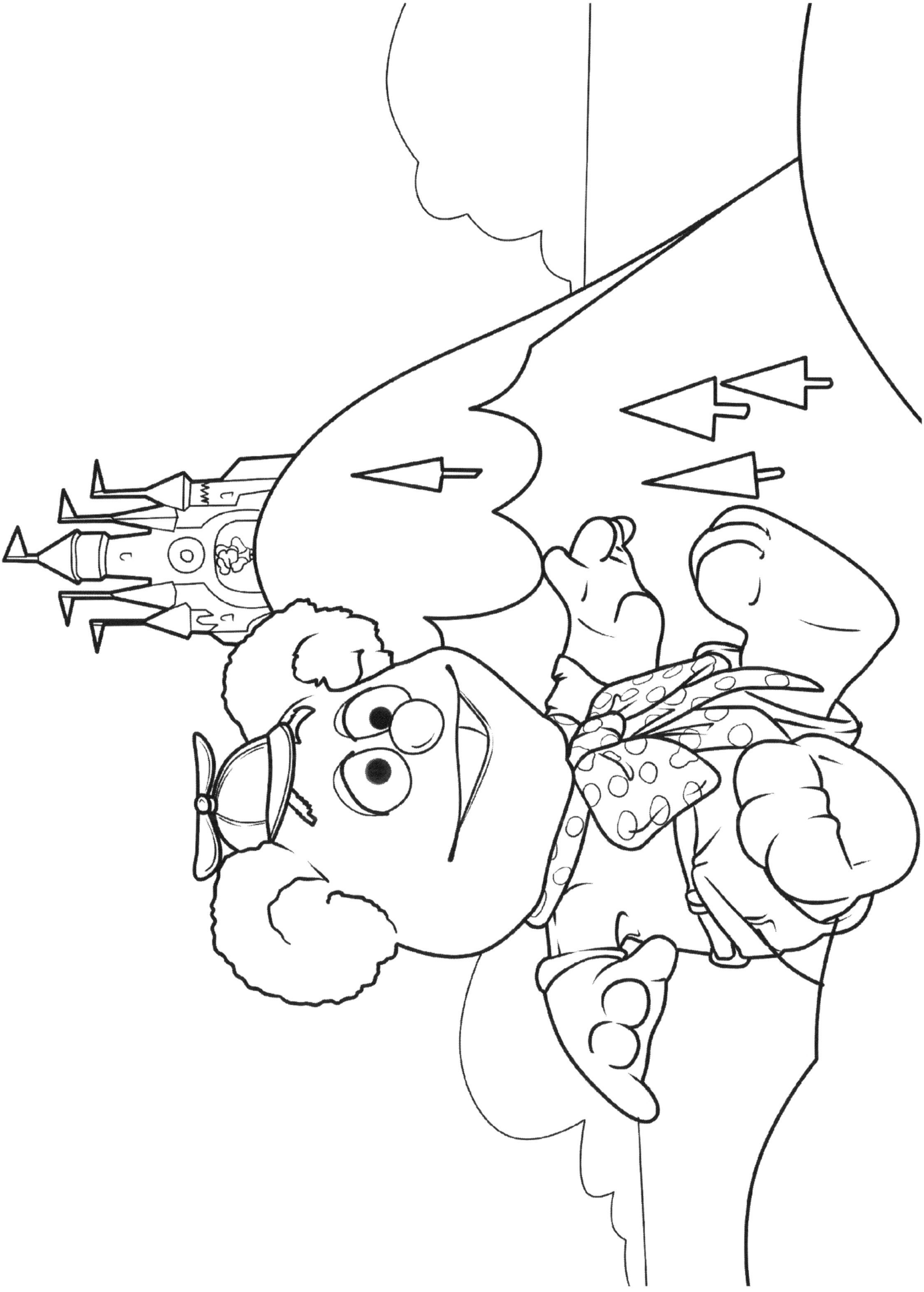

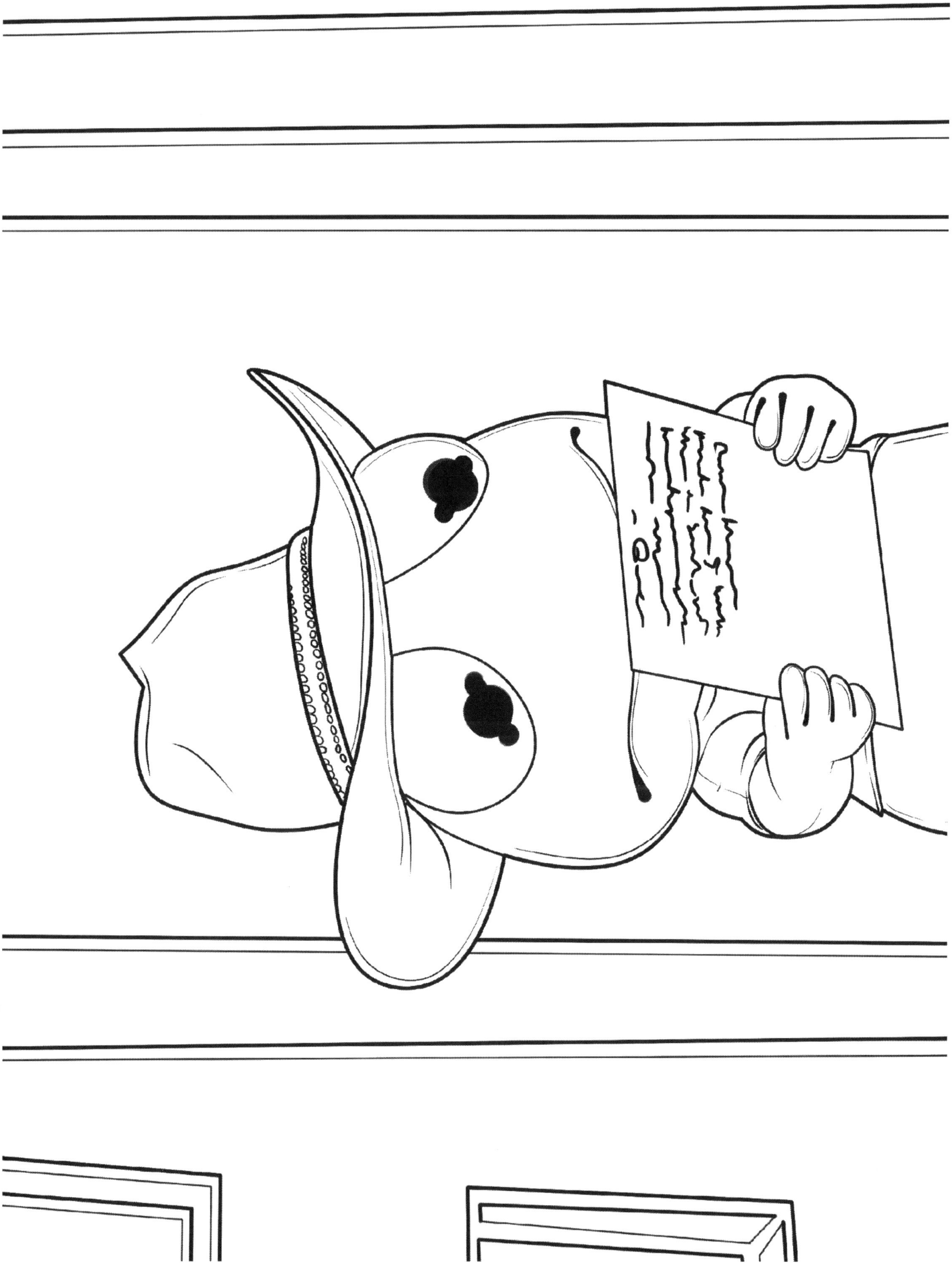

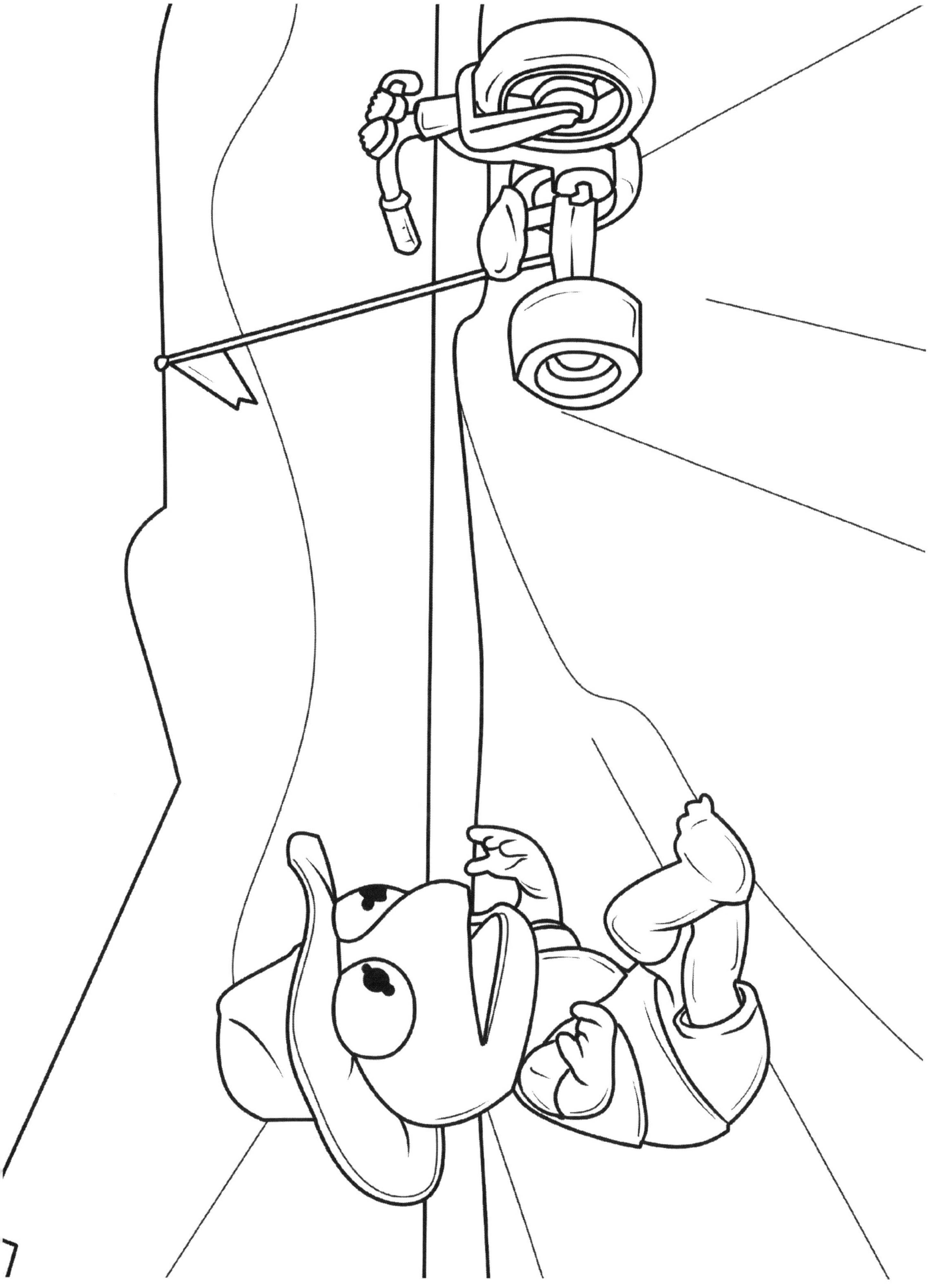

48422619R00069

Made in the USA
San Bernardino, CA
16 August 2019